Linco

Fields

Jeffer
Lincoln Inn Fields

Lincoln
Inn

New Market

Clemens

Assurance House

Stronde

at the Horse

Somerset
house

Exeter

Somerset Yarde

Worcester Yard

Durham Yard

Waterhouse

Durhell Staires

Iford Staires

THE BRITISH MUSEUM
LONDON

Great Russell Street with the gateway of the British Museum (detail), 1778, watercolour by Michael Angelo Rooker (1743–1801)

THE BRITISH MUSEUM
LONDON

Sheila O'Connell

THE BRITISH MUSEUM PRESS

Endpapers: Map of West London (detail), about 1660,
etching by Wenceslaus Hollar (1607–77)

Photography by the British Museum Department of Photography and
Imaging (Ivor Kerslake)
Additional commissioned photography by Jeremy Stafford-Deitsch

© 2004 The Trustees of the British Museum
First published in 2004 by The British Museum Press
A division of The British Museum Company Ltd
46 Bloomsbury Street, London WC1B 3QQ

Sheila O'Connell has asserted her moral right to be identified
as the author of this work
A catalogue record for this book is available from the British Library

ISBN 0 7141 5013 4

Designed and typeset in Centaur by Peter Ward
Printed in China by C&C Offset

CONTENTS

INTRODUCTION

7

THE CITY

10

THE WEST END

23

WESTMINSTER

42

THE RIVER THAMES

52

RURAL LONDON

64

TRAVELLING IN LONDON

80

ILLUSTRATION REFERENCES

96

'London', a page from the illuminated book
Songs of Experience, 1794, by William Blake (1757–1827)

INTRODUCTION

T HE BRITISH MUSEUM'S collection encompasses material from cities as distant as ancient Ur and modern Dhaka, and deals with cultures from the Amazon to the Nile, from Easter Island to the Cyclades. But this book looks closer to home where, far from ignoring its local heritage, the Museum houses many hundreds of views of London. Among the most important examples are more than a thousand prints and drawings bequeathed by John Charles Crowle in 1811, six thousand items purchased from the family of Frederick Crace in 1880, a magnificent group of prints and drawings by Wenceslaus Hollar, hundreds of drawings of early nineteenth-century London by George Scharf, and many individual items by artists as renowned as Giovanni Antonio Canaletto, J. M. W. Turner and John Constable.

This book offers forty-five views of London – watercolours, drawings and prints from the Museum's collection, and photographs specially commissioned to show complementary aspects of London today. Artists whose work is represented include George Cruikshank, who was born in what is now Coptic Street, Bloomsbury; Thomas Rowlandson, born in the City; and Turner (Covent Garden) and William Blake (Soho). Thomas Girtin was born in Southwark and moved across the river to the City when still a child. But this book also includes views of London by a Bohemian, an Italian, a Bavarian, an American and two French artists, all of whom lived in London. The Japanese printmakers responsible for two somewhat surprising London views never actually came here – their woodcuts are based on photographs and prints published in illustrated magazines. More direct intervention from overseas is shown in a modern photograph of Chinatown, an area of central London which has been transformed in recent decades.

Most artists show London as they and their patrons would have hoped to see it — a well-ordered city with cloudless skies. London's history is celebrated in Wenceslaus Hollar's view of the Tower, in Canaletto's drawing of old London Bridge just before its shops and houses were swept away in 1758, in Turner's interior of Westminster Abbey, in Thomas Sandby's sweep of Whitehall with the elaborate sixteenth-century gateway said to be (but probably not) designed by Hans Holbein for Henry VIII (and also to be demolished in the modernizing 1750s). Eighty years later, David Roberts suffused the Westminster riverside and the Banqueting Hall with a nostalgic haze. Civic pride is represented in late eighteenth-century watercolours of one of Wren's City churches and one of the grand Mayfair squares. London's modernity is the theme of James Pollard's proud depiction of the age of coaching, of Cyril Power's underground train as a symbol of the Machine Age, and of Jeremy Stafford-Deitsch's photographs of Millennium innovations. Day-to-day life in London appears in views of the old Billingsgate fish market, fruit and vegetable stalls in Covent Garden, shops in a tiny lane behind St Martin-in-the-Fields, and advertising in Cheapside. Town travel is shown dating from the days when the river served as London's 'main street' right up to its modern trademarks of shiny black cabs and red double-decker buses.

Londoners dream of a rural idyll. Until the late eighteenth century the town was still ringed by open fields and market gardens, and on summer evenings people would stroll out to the villages of Chelsea, Bayswater or Islington. Further out, we see rural Willesden in the 1820s, and Plumstead Common saved from development in the 1870s. Hampstead on its hill has always enjoyed clean air and fine views.

Richmond, discovered by medieval monarchs, remains an upriver resort for Londoners. Public parks and private gardens play a vital role at all levels of society. The garden front of Buckingham House (later Palace) looking westwards, away from the smoke and grime of the capital, was lettered with the words RUS IN URBE (the country within the town). Edward Dayes shows fashionable Londoners of the 1790s promenading in St James's Park with the east front of Buckingham House behind them. Charles Ginner focuses on a tiny breathing space near Charing Cross, while Frank Auerbach shows the welcome green of Primrose Hill.

But some artists cannot escape urban hardship. William Blake's poem 'London' is ineffably bleak. His image of an old man helped by a lively child contrasts with the verses, where he looks around him at the dreadful fate of the young in a corrupt and venial city. By contrast, Gustave Doré's poverty-stricken children in Seven Dials are pretty enough not to frighten his Victorian audience, Rowlandson's fish-wives and watermen are figures of fun, and in Whistler's Wapping the squalor has an elegant line.

The watercolour reproduced on the jacket of this book is one of the British Museum's treasures. It comes from a series of studies made by the short-lived Thomas Girtin for his huge lost panorama of London seen from a high building at the southern end of Blackfriars Bridge — two other watercolours from the series are also shown (pp. 42–3 and 60–1). Some of the buildings seen in Girtin's view survive. Church spires rise above and between more mundane structures, and the River Thames still follows its course, though now between embankments that serve to separate it from the city. On a fine day when the river reflects the light, those who love London are tempted to echo the words of Girtin's contemporary, William Wordsworth: 'Earth has not anything to show more fair'.

THE CITY

THE TOWER is the oldest surviving building in London, erected on the eastern edge of the city by William the Conqueror from 1077 onwards. His purpose was not only to defend London from attack, but also to create a permanent reminder of the power of the monarchy as a warning to independently minded citizens.

The Bohemian printmaker Wenceslaus Hollar spent much of his career in London, and his views of the city are among the greatest of the period. This drawing is related to one of a set of four etchings of London published in 1644. In the 1660s Hollar planned a 10-ft x 5-ft map of London. The only surviving section, which is in the British Museum, is reproduced on the endpapers of this book.

Den Tower van London

The Tower of London, about 1641–4, pen and ink with
watercolour by Wenceslaus Hollar (1607–77)

Overleaf: Old London Bridge, 1750s, pen and ink and wash
by Giovanni Antonio Canaletto (1697–1768)

FEEDING LONDON has always been a major preoccupation, and the great food markets are important landmarks. Billingsgate, just downstream of London Bridge, was the main London fish market from at least the thirteenth century. Its porters and more especially its fish-wives were notorious for their tough manners and bad language.

In this print Rowlandson portrays a group of burly Irishwomen who have made their way from St Giles's, a poverty-stricken area near the British Museum, to load up their baskets with fish that they will sell in the streets for a few pennies. William Hogarth's famous painting of the Shrimp Girl in the National Gallery is a far more sympathetic view of a Billingsgate street vendor. In 1982 the market moved downstream to the Isle of Dogs.

'Procession of the Cod Company from St Giles's to Billingsgate', 1810,
hand-coloured etching by Thomas Rowlandson (1757–1827)

CHEAPSIDE was London's major shopping street from the twelfth century onwards. Its name comes from the Old English word for market. Halfway down the street on the right-hand side rises the tower of St Mary-le-Bow. Only those born within the sound of her Bow bells are said to be true Londoners.

This photograph was published as a postcard by G. Mellin of Peckham to advertise Mellin's Food ('a simple nourishing diet for a baby or an aged person'). The image was doctored so that signs advertising the product appear prominently, for instance on the motorbus in the foreground. The card is part of a collection of a million trade cards bequeathed to the British Museum in 1995 by Edward Wharton-Tigar.

Cheapside, about 1900, hand-coloured photograph (anonymous)

LONDON: CHEAPSIDE, LOOKING E.

THIS WATERCOLOUR shows the elegant church of St Lawrence Jewry, one of many rebuilt by Christopher Wren after the Great Fire of 1666. In the background is the Guildhall, home of the Corporation of London since the twelfth century. Recent excavations have revealed that the buildings occupy the site of the great amphitheatre of Roman London.

Thomas Malton specialized in architectural subjects, especially views of London, which was developing during his lifetime as the capital of a world-wide empire. Between 1792 and 1801, Malton published a series of one hundred prints based on drawings like this one, catering to blossoming civic pride with views of famous London landmarks.

St Lawrence Jewry and the Guildhall, 1783,
watercolour by Thomas Malton (1748–1804)

THE FIRST St Paul's is thought to have been begun in the year 604 on one of the highest sites in the city. A series of rebuildings followed until the fourth (medieval) cathedral was devastated by the Great Fire of 1666. Its magnificent replacement was designed by Christopher Wren and took thirty-five years to build at a cost of nearly £750,000. Completed in 1710, it is one of the great sights of London. The dome still dominates the City. In the crypt is Wren's simple epitaph in Latin: Reader, if you seek his monument, look around you.

The dome of St Paul's Cathedral photographed from the south bank of the Thames, viewed across one of London's newest landmarks, the Millennium Bridge leading from Tate Modern to the City.

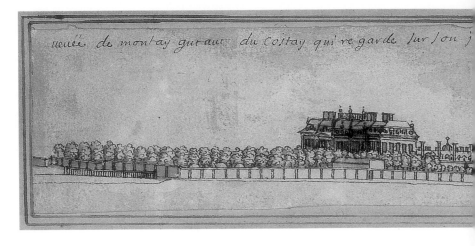

neuée de montay qui aux du Coftay qui re garde fur fon j

Montagu House from the north, about 1700, pen and ink with wash
by François(?) Gasselin (active about 1683–1703)

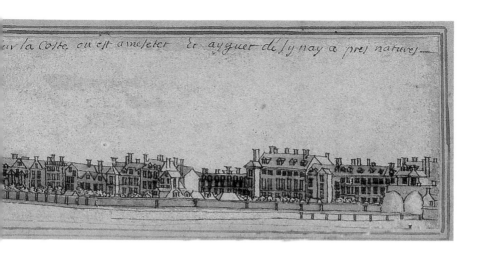

THE WEST END

THIS DRAWING looks across open fields to the backs of houses in Great Russell Street, then the northern border of London. In the centre is Montagu House, which was to open in 1759 as the first home of the British Museum. The artist has described the view in phonetic French: *veuéé de montay gue aue du costay qui re garde sur son jardin et sur la coste ou est amesetet et ayguet désynay a pres natures* (view of Montagu House from the side which looks towards its garden and the side where are Hampstead and Highgate, drawn from nature).

Gasselin was evidently a member of the Huguenot Protestant community which came to England at the end of the seventeenth century seeking refuge from persecution in France, but little is known about him and even his first name is uncertain.

THIS COLOUR woodcut comes from a novel in fifteen volumes telling the comic adventures of two ordinary men from the back streets of Edo (modern Tokyo) who make a journey to London. The British Museum is shown here in a view that was probably based on photographs or prints that had found their way to Japan. Statues have been added on either side of the gateway, and the skyline is enlivened with spires and a palm tree growing in the forecourt.

The British Museum,
from *Shanks's Mare around the
West* (*Seiyō dōchū hizakurige*),
1870–6, colour woodcut by
Utagawa Yoshiiku (1833–1904),
Utagawa Hiroshige III
(1843–94) and Kawanabe
Kyōsai (1831–89)

Overleaf: Covent Garden Market, 1825, watercolour
by George Scharf (1788–1860)

JUST A QUARTER of a mile south of the British Museum is Seven Dials, notorious throughout the eighteenth and nineteenth centuries as one of the poorest areas of London. It is shown here in a wood-engraving designed by Gustave Doré to accompany Blanchard Jerrold's text in *London: A Pilgrimage*.

Charles Dickens Junior wrote in the late 1870s: 'Here poverty is to be seen in its most painful features. The shops sell nothing but second or third hand articles – old dresses, old clothes, old hats, and at the top of the stairs of little underground cellars, old shoes, so patched and mended that it is questionable whether one particle of the original material remains in them.' Up to thirty people were recorded as living in each of the houses shown here. Dudley Street was demolished in the 1880s for the construction of Shaftesbury Avenue.

Dudley Street, Seven Dials, 1872, wood-engraving designed by Gustave Doré (1832–83)

THE STRAND runs parallel to the Thames from the western boundary of the City. In the Middle Ages it was lined with the grand town houses of ruling families, but by the end of the seventeenth century aristocratic London had moved further west and the area around the Strand became the lively centre of the entertainment industry.

In the 1670s the old mansion of the Earls of Exeter was demolished and on its site was erected Exeter Change, with a two-storey arcade of shops. From 1773 to 1829 it housed a famous menagerie, shown in this watercolour, which included lions, tigers, monkeys, a hippopotamus, a sloth and a 5-ton elephant named Chunee.

The Strand, 1815, watercolour
by George Shepherd (1784–1862)

CHARLES GINNER was a leading figure in the Camden Town Group of artists established in 1911. His deadpan, carefully observed views of London exude a feeling of restrained intensity. This watercolour depicts a small public park near Charing Cross, where a couple sit engrossed in conversation. The grand structure behind them is York Water Gate, erected in 1626 to give access to the Thames from York House, the London mansion of George Villiers, Duke of Buckingham and a favourite of King James I. The York Water Gate is now separated from the river by 150 metres of land reclaimed from the muddy shore when the Victoria Embankment was built in the 1860s.

Victoria Embankment Gardens, 1920s, watercolour
by Charles Ginner (1878–1952)

THE BAVARIAN artist George Scharf came to England after serving with the British Army at the Battle of Waterloo in 1815. He spent the rest of his life in London, living for many years in a street just to the north of the British Museum, and 1400 of his sketches of everyday life in the rapidly changing city came to the Museum from his family.

This watercolour shows Church Lane, a narrow court to the east of the church of St Martin-in-the-Fields, which was to be swept away as part of the 1830s improvements to the western end of the Strand. Scharf's watercolour view of Covent Garden (pp. 26–7) was made only three years before the ramshackle wooden stalls were replaced by the present colonnaded market building in 1828.

Church Lane with St Martin-in-the-Fields, July 1828, watercolour by George Scharf (1788–1860)

Overleaf: Piccadilly was built up from the late seventeenth century onwards. The Earl of Burlington's mansion of the 1660s survives, much remodelled, behind the Victorian façade of the Royal Academy of Arts

near St Martins Church July 1828

MAYFAIR is an eighteenth-century creation, built by aristocratic landowners on what had been open fields to the west of London. Hanover Square was the first of the Mayfair squares, laid out between 1717 and 1719 and named in honour of the new Hanoverian dynasty. It has always been a desirable address – by 1725 the parish contained nine dukes, two marquesses, twenty-one earls, six viscounts, thirteen barons and two bishops. In this watercolour, made towards the end of the century, the scene is enlivened by street vendors, horsemen and an extraordinarily well-sprung carriage carrying a lady in a fashionable feathered hat.

Hanover Square, 1787, watercolour by Edward Dayes (1763–1804) and Robert Thew (1758–1802)

London's Chinatown began to develop only in the 1950s. The Chinese community in the dockland area of Limehouse had been largely bombed out in the Second World War and was seeking affordable accommodation. A new source of income was also needed, as employment at sea became harder to find and traditional Chinese laundries were superseded by domestic washing machines. The run-down area adjacent to London's theatreland, where property prices were low, was the ideal place to develop a new market for Chinese cuisine.

The population grew as immigrants from Hong Kong arrived after the Chinese Communist revolution of 1949. By the end of the 1970s, the area between Shaftesbury Avenue and Leicester Square was almost entirely taken over by Chinese businesses, and the street signs are now in both Chinese and English. The Chinese New Year celebrations in late January or early February have become an important date in London's calendar.

Eighteenth-century Gerrard Street has been transformed into the bustling heart of Chinatown

WESTMINSTER

THIS IS A STUDY for Girtin's great lost panorama of London (108 feet long and 18 feet high), completed in August 1802. William Wordsworth's 'On Westminster Bridge' was written a month later:

Earth has not anything to show more fair:
Dull would he be of soul who could pass by
A sight so touching in its majesty:
This City now doth, like a garment, wear
The beauty of the morning; silent, bare,
Ships, towers, domes, theatres, and temples lie
Open unto the fields, and to the sky;
All bright and glittering in the smokeless air.
Never did sun more beautifully steep
In his first splendour, valley, rock, or hill;
Ne'er saw I, never felt, a calm so deep!
The river glideth at his own sweet will:
Dear God! the very houses seem asleep;
And all that mighty heart is lying still!

A distant view of Westminster from the south, 1801, watercolour
by Thomas Girtin (1775–1802). Girtin made several other watercolours
for the same project (pp. 60–1 and jacket illustration)

Turner was twenty-one when he exhibited this large watercolour at the Royal Academy. He was already going beyond the straightforward descriptive watercolour tradition in which he had been trained and was pushing the medium to create the sort of dramatic effects usually seen only in oil paintings. Here he takes a viewpoint at the east end of Westminster Abbey, focusing on the elaborate Islip chapel of the 1520s. Medieval architecture appealed to the late eighteenth-century taste for the picturesque, but Turner's achievement was to recreate the atmosphere of the great church, with its soaring vaults and light pouring into its deep shadows.

The Interior of Westminster Abbey, 1796, watercolour
by Joseph Mallord William Turner (1775–1851)

THIS PHOTOGRAPH includes one of London's most famous sights, the Clock Tower of the Palace of Westminster (the Houses of Parliament) – known around the world by the name of its bell, Big Ben. The tower was completed in 1856 as part of the rebuilding of the Houses of Parliament after the fire of 1834. Westminster Hall, whose roof is shown here, is one of the few survivals of the medieval royal palace. It was built between 1097 and 1099 as an extension to the palace built fifty years earlier by King Edward the Confessor. From the thirteenth century until 1882 it housed the Law Courts.

Oliver Cromwell was installed as Lord Protector in Westminster Hall in 1653, four years after Charles I had been condemned to death there. This bronze statue by Hamo Thornycroft, showing Cromwell holding a bible in one hand and a sword in the other, was erected in 1899.

Big Ben with the roof of Westminster Hall
and the statue of Oliver Cromwell

Overleaf: Whitehall with the Holbein Gate, about 1750,
watercolour by Thomas Sandby (1723–98)

S<small>T</small> J<small>AMES'S</small> P<small>ARK</small>, to the west of Whitehall, was opened to the public by Charles II and became a place for elegant promenading. The fashionable crowd shown in this large hand-coloured etching is gathered at the far end of the Park in front of Buckingham House, the principal London residence of the royal family since 1762. From 1825 onwards the early eighteenth-century house was rebuilt as Buckingham Palace. The enlargement was instigated by George IV, but the present front facing St James's Park was erected during the reign of Queen Victoria.

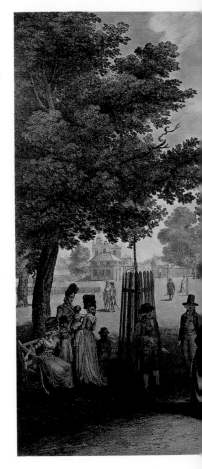

The Promenade in St James's Park, 1793, hand-coloured etching by
François David Soiron (1764–after 1796) after Edward Dayes (1763–1804)

THE RIVER
THAMES

'THE COURT used to take the water from the stairs at Whitehall Palace in summer evenings when the heat and dust prevented their walking in the Park. An infinite number of open boats filled with the Court and City beauties attended the barges in which were the royal family; collations, music and fireworks completed the scene'.

The Count of Grammont's wistful memoir of the court of Charles II is echoed in Roberts's watercolour, dominated by the Banqueting House, sole survivor of the old Palace. The London river scene has an almost Venetian air, with dignified buildings reflected in smooth water and boats that might be gondolas tied up by the shore.

The Westminster riverside, 1831, watercolour
by David Roberts (1796–1864)

CITY HALL opened in July 2002 as home to the new Mayor of London, the London Assembly and the Greater London Authority. It is part of the revitalization of the south bank of the Thames and serves as a new landmark close to one of London's most famous sights, Tower Bridge.

The gothic bridge was completed in 1894 to provide a river crossing for the huge population of the booming eastern side of London. Since the Port of London extended upstream of Tower Bridge, it was designed with an ingenious seesaw mechanism so that the roadway could be raised in one minute to allow large ships to pass through. Tower Bridge is still raised some 900 times each year.

Tower Bridge, a great Victorian engineering feat, viewed from beside the new City Hall, built just over a century later

S HERLOCK made a number of watercolours of the outskirts of London. Here the riverside road running along the north bank from Westminster to Chelsea is still a picturesque, if muddy, track, with a rural appearance. But within a few years the area was to undergo drastic change. In 1811 an iron bridge was built across the Thames to Vauxhall and in 1813 work began on the fortress-like edifice of Millbank Prison, now the site of Tate Britain.

Millbank, about 1800, watercolour by
William Sherlock (active 1800–20)

RICHMOND is sixteen miles west by river from London. It was already a royal resort 750 years ago, and wealthy Londoners built houses there near Richmond Palace. Tudor and Stuart monarchs held tournaments and hunted. The eighteenth century saw a flourishing spa, the founding of a theatre and in 1770 a bridge across the Thames. By Turner's time, Richmond was a favourite place for summer outings from London.

This watercolour belonged to Turner's great champion, John Ruskin. It was Ruskin's first Turner drawing and when he exhibited it in 1878 he gave it the subtitle 'Play' to contrast with the artist's dark watercolour of heavily industrialized Dudley in Worcestershire, which Ruskin called 'Work'.

Richmond Hill and Bridge, about 1829, watercolour
by Joseph Mallord William Turner (1775–1851)

59

View across the Thames from Lambeth to Somerset House, 1801,
watercolour by Thomas Girtin (1775–1802)

I N 1859 the American artist Whistler lived for a few weeks in the dock area of Wapping, just east of the Tower of London. This etching is one of a group of eight Thames subjects that he published twelve years later. A *Punch* reviewer described 'tumble-down bankside buildings . . . where all is pitchy and tarry, and corny and coally, and ancient and fishlike'. Whistler delights in the picturesque squalor of the warehouse buildings, but at the same time brings a new realism to his depiction of the seamen and dockers who take centre stage in these compositions. Thomas Rowlandson made an earlier anecdotal view of the watermen of Wapping (p. 81).

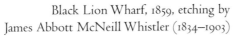

Black Lion Wharf, 1859, etching by
James Abbott McNeill Whistler (1834–1903)

RURAL LONDON

THIS INFORMAL watercolour is one of a number that Barret made of the rural districts around London. Here he shows the charming village of Willesden with its medieval church, St Mary's. The area remained largely undeveloped until overtaken by industrialization in the 1880s. St Mary's survives, much restored, but the roads are now choked with traffic.

Willesden, 1826, watercolour by
George Barret (1767–1842)

The village of Bayswater, 1793, watercolour
by Paul Sandby (1730–1809)

Overleaf: St James's Park, Green Park (shown here), Hyde Park and Kensington Gardens together provide some 750 acres of open landscape in the heart of London, interrupted only by the traffic island of Hyde Park Corner

EVEN TODAY Hampstead, with its acres of open heath and narrow streets, retains a hint of its village past, though the centre of London is visible from its heights. On the back of this watercolour Constable noted that he drew it at 12 noon on a day in September 1830 from the drawing room of his house at no. 6 Well Walk, Hampstead. Three years earlier he had written, 'Our little drawing room commands a view unequalled in Europe — from Westminster Abbey to Gravesend — the dome of St Paul's in the air realises Michelangelo's idea on seeing that of the Pantheon — "I will build such a thing in the sky".' From 1830 onwards Constable became concerned to capture the transitory effects of moving clouds in a series of small watercolours like this one.

London from Hampstead, 1830, watercolour
by John Constable (1776–1837)

Inner London is ringed by residential developments of the 1820s and 30s. To modern eyes these terraces have a characteristic appeal, but contemporaries lamented the loss of the open fields that had been within walking distance of town. In this print Cruikshank shows bricks, mortar, chimneys and builders' tools driving out the rural delights of sheep, cattle, hay-ricks, fences and trees. Brick-kilns spew out their products and in the background clouds of smoke spread over the countryside. It is ironic that Cruikshank himself lived in a new house in Islington, not unlike those he portrays here.

'London going out of Town – or – The March of Bricks & Mortar!',
1829, hand-coloured etching by George Cruikshank (1792–1878)

R.B.Schnebbelie. 1839

THE TREES of St John's Wood were only cut down in the mid seventeenth century and for nearly two hundred years its market gardens and grassy meadows remained an important source of sustenance for London. Middle-class villas were built in pleasant gardens. From 1812 Regent's Park was developed to the southeast and in 1814 Thomas Lord moved his cricket ground to St John's Wood.

This watercolour shows a crowd gathering to watch a balloon ascent by George Graham and his wife Margaret in 1839. The first balloon ascents took place in France in 1783 and rapidly became a favourite attraction at pleasure gardens and other open spaces on the edge of London. The Grahams made numerous ascents between 1823 and 1852.

Balloon Ascent at Lord's Cricket Ground, 1839, watercolour by Robert Bremmel Schnebbelie (active 1803–49)

Gross's watercolour shows Plumstead Common in southeast London, with a street of houses called The Slade and the attractively named Ravine Grove. Until the mid nineteenth century Plumstead remained a prosperous rural village, with sheep grazing on the marshes to the north and fruit growing on the hilly land to the south. Spreading industrial development and the coming of the railways threatened to engulf the area until in the 1870s Plumstead and Winns Commons were acquired by the Metropolitan Board of Works and preserved as public open spaces.

John Betjeman, poet of twentieth-century London, declared in 1947 that Gross's Fulham street-scenes were 'the most gratifying delineations of the London suburbs that I have seen'. Gross moved from Chelsea to south-east London in 1959, and thereafter his work reflected the panoramic views across the rooftops from Greenwich Hill and other vantage points.

Plumstead, 1965, watercolour by Anthony Gross (1905- 84)

The fields from Islington to Marybone,
To Primrose Hill and Saint John's Wood,
Were builded over with pillars of gold;
And there Jerusalem's pillars stood.

Her Little Ones ran on the fields,
The Lamb of God among them seen,
And fair Jerusalem, his Bride,
Among the little meadows green.

Pancras and Kentish town repose
Among her golden pillars high,
Among her golden arches which
Shine upon the starry sky.

The Jews's Harp House and the Green Man,
The Ponds where Boys to bathe delight,
The fields of Cows by William's farm,
Shine in Jerusalem's pleasant sight.

From 'Liberty' by William Blake (1757–1827)

Primrose Hill, 1974, watercolour with gouache
and graphite by Frank Auerbach (b. 1931)

TRAVELLING IN LONDON

THE RIVER THAMES has been called the main street of London. In the early nineteenth century it still provided the most effective means of travel, not only for national and international trade, but also within the town itself. Watermen — the taxi-drivers of their day — were licensed to carry passengers across and up and down the river, and they were famous for plying their trade with gusto. In this print Rowlandson depicts watermen at Wapping vying for the custom of a stout woman who is returning from a shopping trip with her purchases tucked up in her apron. The oval metal badges on their shoulders carried their registration numbers.

'Miseries of London', 1812, hand-coloured etching
by Thomas Rowlandson (1757–1827)

Overleaf: The Port of London (*Igirisu Rondon no kaikō*), 1862,
colour woodcut by Utagawa Yoshitora (active about 1850–80)

WAPPING
OLD STAIRS

MISERIES of LONDON.

Entering upon any of the bridges of London, or any of the passages leading to the Thames, being assailed by a groupe of watermen, holding up their hands and bawling out. Oars Sculls, Sculls, Oars, Oars.

Designed Pub.d July 12 1112 by T. Rowlandson N.o James S.t Adelphi.

Befell that in that season on a day,
In Southwark at the Tabard as I lay
Ready to wenden on my pilgrimage . . .

IT WAS AT THIS INN, in the late fourteenth century, that Geoffrey Chaucer had his pilgrims spend the night before setting off for Canterbury, and it was the landlord who suggested that they pass their time by recounting tales as they rode. In the early nineteenth century the Talbot — as it was by then called — was one of many inns lining the route south from London Bridge. Roads had improved vastly in the eighteenth century and coaches and waggons, like the ones shown in this watercolour, carried people and goods around the country, but they were soon to be superseded by the railway. The Talbot was demolished in the 1870s.

The Talbot Inn, Southwark, about 1820,
watercolour by George Shepherd
(1784–1862)

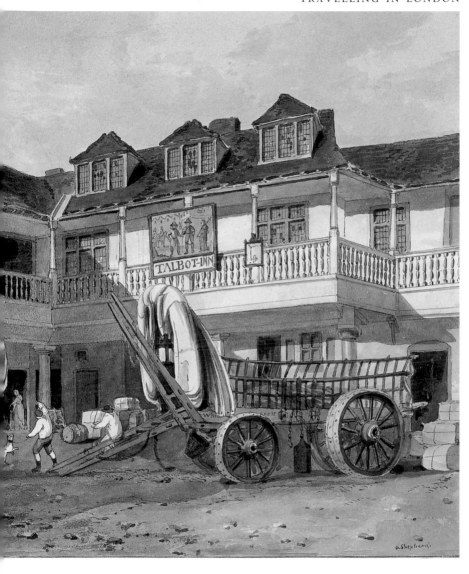

ROBERT SMIRKE designed the General Post Office, just north of St Paul's Cathedral, at the same time as he was rebuilding the British Museum with a similarly grand Greek Ionic colonnade. Charles Dickens has the north-country John Browdie declare in *Nicholas Nickleby*: 'if thot's on'y a Poast Office, I'd loike to see where the Lord Mayor o' Lunnon lives'.

Hand-coloured aquatints designed by James Pollard epitomize the great age of coaching. Here we see the departure of the mail coaches which left London every evening punctually at 8 pm, loaded with passengers from the great inns that served as termini and with mail collected from the General Post Office. By the early 1830s, both Exeter and Manchester could be reached in a day.

The General Post Office, London, 1830, hand-coloured aquatint by Richard Gilson Reeve (1803–89) after James Pollard (1792–1867)

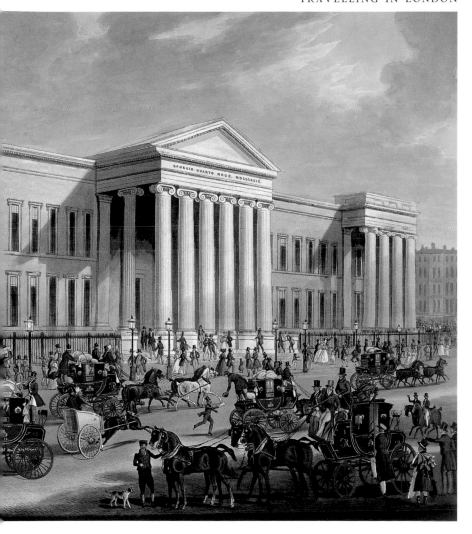

Overleaf: St Mary-le-Strand, designed by James Gibbs and consecrated in 1724, now surrounded by the familiar sights of modern London traffic

K ING'S CROSS railway station was built in 1851–2 as the London terminus of the Great Northern Railway, catering for trains running between the capital and Lincolnshire and Yorkshire. Trains from Birmingham arrived half a mile to the west, at Euston (built in 1837). In between, St Pancras Station was built in 1863–8 for trains from Derby. The shabby suburbs that had formerly lain to the north of Euston Road were swept away for these mighty developments.

The huge dustheap shown in this drawing, largely created by ashes from brickworks in Gray's Inn Road, had been a feature of the area for a hundred years. When it was removed in the 1840s to clear the site for the new King's Cross Station, rumours circulated that the material was to be shipped to Russia to help in the rebuilding of Moscow after the Napoleonic invasion.

View of the Great Dustheap. It was removed in 1848 to has been built on the s

The Great Dustheap at King's Cross, 1840,
watercolour by E. H. Dixon (active 1840–59)

Between 1926 and 1937 Cyril Power made some forty-five linocuts, many of which depict images of the Machine Age. This print was inspired by the rush hour trains on the District Line at Hammersmith, where Power had a studio during the 1930s. He creates a dynamic pattern of repeated angular forms and sharp contrasts of tone. The elegantly dressed commuters, each shielded by the day's newspaper, appear as automata swept up in the relentless movement of the modern city.

The Tube Train, about 1934,
linocut by Cyril Power (1872–1951)

THE LONDON EYE rises above all but the highest office buildings and provides a spectacular view of the city and its suburbs. Originally known as the Millennium Wheel, it was erected as part of the celebrations and has since become a favourite attraction for Londoners and visitors alike.

From the Eye one can see a modern version of Thomas Girtin's panorama of two centuries ago (pp. 42–3, 60–1 and jacket illustration), retrace Hollar's seventeenth-century map of London (endpapers) and feel the same excitement as the passengers in Mr Graham's balloon as it soared into the sky above the city in the mid 1800s (pp. 74–5).

The London Eye, designed by architects Julia Barfield and David Marks, opened in 2000 and is the tallest observation wheel in the world: at 135 metres high, it weighs 1700 tonnes

ILLUSTRATION REFERENCES

Photographs © The Trustees of the British Museum, courtesy of the Departments of Prints and Drawings (PD) or Asia unless otherwise noted.

page

2   PD 1868-3-28-334

6   PD 1924-7-26-2(19) (Presented by Mrs B. B. Macgeorge)

11   PD 1859-8-6-389

12–13   PD 1909-4-6-4

14–15   PD 1872-10-12-4961

17   PD WT Box 160 Mellin (Bequeathed by Edward Wharton-Tigar)

18–19   PD 1880-11-13-3594

21   Jeremy Stafford-Deitsch

22–3   PD 1860-7-14-4

24–5   Asia 2001-5-8-01 (Purchased with the support of the BM Friends)

26–7   PD 1862-6-14-31

28–9   PD 1979-4-7-16(46) 162.d.5

31   PD 1907-10-18-40

33   PD 1934-2-27-1 (Presented anonymously; © the artist's estate)

35   PD 1862-6-14-107

36–7   Jeremy Stafford-Deitsch

38–9   PD 1880-11-13-4535

41   Jeremy Stafford-Deitsch

42–3   PD 1855-2-14-23 (Presented by Chambers Hall)

45   PD 1958-7-12-402 (Bequeathed by R. W. Lloyd)

47   Jeremy Stafford-Deitsch

48–9   PD 1941-6-18-1 (Presented by National Art Collections Fund)

50–1   PD 1880-11-13-2349

52–3   PD 2002-3-23-11 (Presented through the National Art Collections Fund by Professor Luke Hermann (from the Bruce Ingram collection))

page

55   Jeremy Stafford-Deitsch

56–7   PD 1862-12-13-58

58–9   PD 1958-7-12-435 (Bequeathed by R. W. Lloyd)

60–1   PD 1855-2-14-27 (Presented by Chambers Hall)

62–3   PD 1973-9-15-15

64–5   PD 1910-2-18-25 (Presented by Mrs Robert Law)

66–7   PD 1904-8-19-67 (Bequeathed by William Sandby)

68–9   Jeremy Stafford-Deitsch

71   PD 1888-2-15-50 (Presented by Miss Isabel Constable)

73   PD 1978.u.1616 (Bequeathed by Mrs Eliza Cruikshank)

74–5   PD 1879-8-9-652

76–7   PD 1967-12-9-6 (© the artist's estate)

79   PD 1981-6-20-16 (© the artist)

81   PD 1876-10-14-14

82–3   Asia 1906-12-20-1347

84–5   PD K.67-100

86–7   PD 1917-12-8-2253 (Presented by Baroness Lucas of Crudwell and Dingwall in memory of her brother the 8th Baron Lucas)

88–9   Jeremy Stafford-Deitsch

90–1   PD 1871-8-12-5659

92–3   PD 1985-10-5-21 (© the artist's estate)

95   Jeremy Stafford-Deitsch

endpapers   PD Q.6-136

jacket   PD 1855-2-14-28 (Presented by Chambers Hall)

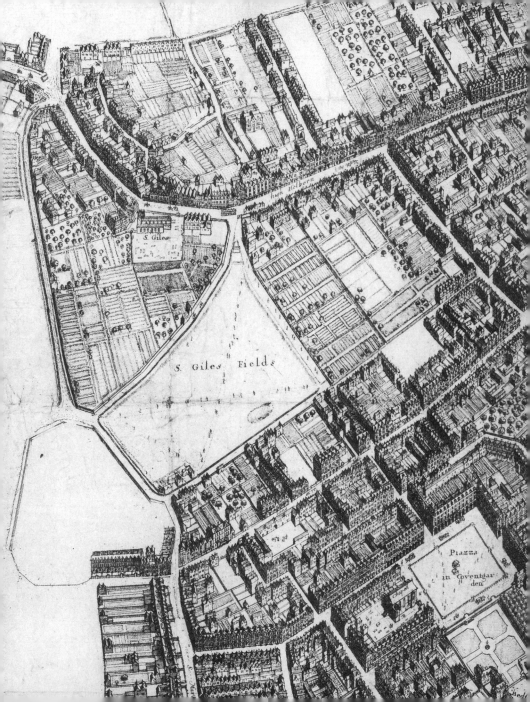